Conjugated Visits

Conjugated Visits

poems

Diane Kirsten Martin

Dream Horse Press
California

Library of Congress Cataloging-in-Publication Data:

Martin, Diane Kirsten
        Conjugated Visits
                p.   cm

                ISBN 978-1-935716-01-3
                1. Poetry

10 9 8 7 6 5 4 3 2 1

First Edition

Cover: "Ravens" by John F. Martin.

For John

Amor, ch'a nullo amato amar perdona,
mi prese del costui piacer sì forte,
che, come vedi, ancor non m'abbandona.

Dante, *Divina Commedia, Inferno* V.82-142
 (Paolo & Francesca)

Contents

Bequest

Small Talk

Conjugated Visits

Lucknow, India — Scientists find 65-million-year-old slime mold fused in sexual union. "The sexual organs being delicate and the time of conjugation short lived, it is indeed rare to get this stage in the fossil state," the study said.

Sonhar

I can't translate the blue of wisteria.
There are many things of which we could not speak —

that he held me down to blue carpet, lips crushed
by obdurate teeth, that seven

different purples populate the garden;
it's the blue I need.

It was so cold that winter, he could never warm me.
My lips were blue. We were afraid, I think.

This is not about the color of memory.
I could make up something more true.

My blood. His fingers.
Blood has the salinity of oceans but is warmer.

Dried lavender smells so blue,
bees will visit the memory.

What is the Portuguese for dreaming?
The purpose of memory?

What of the friend who stops me (blue light, a hallway) —
He wants you. Why do you not go to him?

Conjugated Visits

I love as if it mattered:
a pound of love's feathers falling
fast as a pound of stone.

You love like a weed, unwanted:
taking up residence, calling
it home.

She loves as a snail would:
using him up for sustenance,
leaving a trail.

He loves like the rabbit pulled
from a hat: pedaling,
ambushed by thin air.

We love as the blind see: aware
of insect wings, timbre
the dog hears.

Love dusted treetops,
gutters, and hood ornaments;
she inhaled.

Love contained him
comfortably, a soft shoe;
on firmament he danced.

There would be no way
they could unlove, unspice
the condiment,

uncook the stew, the braised
beast unslaughter, send it
ululating back to the herd.

Demimonde

She writes with lavender ink on cream vellum. A crow
takes roost in the monkey puzzle, is lost

in its formal bracts. It rains; the rivers rise.
Clouds drifting east swell with the monsoon

flooding Thailand; the woman weeps
as she writes. A cargo liner headed seaward

escapes the tip of a triangle. Fingers of rain
point down. A foghorn declaims the enormity

of ocean, its black fathoms. In a small town
on another coast, a man checks the sky,

puts on his raincoat, opens his mailbox — galvanized steel,
flag for rural delivery — inside, an envelope

that he slices with the knife he folds
and pockets before removing her letter.

He will know the spidery purple, the fine cream,
the strokes that slope left, slightly. See, the ink

on the letter is smudged, *I just need to know
you are there*, the envelope, rain spotted.

Out of the Blue

Robert Johnson drove the last bus back to town.
Nights I worked late, I was the only rider.
He asked me if I knew the blues, his granddad was *the* Robert Johnson.

I knew the bluesman, Robert Johnson,
And the way he was said to carry on —
Every place he played the guitar, he had a woman.

His granddad met the Devil at the crossroads.
The Devil was playing the guitar.
What I would give for that! says Johnson. Devil smiled, *It's yours.*

His granddaddy's whiskey was poisoned on account of a woman.
Bus driver said, "I lead a clean life,
Drive my bus, don't mess around. Bring my paycheck home to the wife."

"My boyfriend plays the blues," I told him,
Thought about trimming the tree alone last night.
Slept on the velvet, claw-foot sofa; next thing I knew it was light.

Outside our bus, the snow had teeth.
Slush puddled under our boots on the floor.
All I saw was my face in the window, couldn't see much more.

"What you want Santa to bring you?" asked Robert Johnson.
I didn't want anything. He shook his head.
"Never knew a woman that doesn't want nothin'," bus driver said.

They Don't Talk All Day Except for Choosing Pumpkins

This one's too tall, this one's flat on one side;
How the ideal is so clear, it obscures the real —
Platonism expanded to the choice of pumpkins.

If only, she thinks. And he, *if only*.
He: *before we moved here*. She: *before the baby*.
While the future was still out there,

visible on the horizon, like the Farallones.
They pose for pictures with a donkey.
They pick red and purple corn.

Autumn gilds the fields. *A stage set*,
she thinks, *Indian summer*.
Up Tunitas Road they drive, leaving

pumpkin expanse at ocean. Late sun
like God through redwood. He stops
the car to walk a ways and pee.

She gets out, chunks closed the door,
checks the back seat where the baby's sleeping,
pink underfoot, fairytale green

coating stumps, boulders. *How long
he was gone! But he's back now.*
See, a tender fog swaddles them.

From the Files

Claire blamed the divorce on the therapist.
Before seeing her, Marc seemed vaguely unhappy,
walking around the house as if dragging a trawl net,
unearthing things in its wake. These things,
ugly bottomfish, disturbed their slumber,
roiled and revolved, and occasionally surfaced.

How possessive she is, one of them croaked.
Said another, *a man needs his space*. But mostly
the disgruntlings just floated, as vague things do,
spouting green bile like vacationing gargoyles,
but not roosting on Claire's back. This all changed
when the therapist took Marc's side, Claire thought.

Now all the vaguelings became words. Words
were corporeal, Claire knew. They wheezed
and stank. Their skin was leathery and their teeth
sharp. They gnawed on flesh; in it they would breed.
Once borne into the atmosphere, they would
multiply and could not ever be put back.

An Essay on Marriage

Alone at a JFK gate during a layover, I watch sun through plate glass
refracted by my wedding ring dazzle into peripatetic Tinkerbells,
and I'm suddenly bereft. Once I almost left you over your careless disregard

for the difference between elevators and escalators. One two-year span,
I remember, you didn't say much more than pass the ketchup. But
twenty-three years ago, on a night the red tide entered the bay, we shared

with friends a tent on the sand, each couple old hands at marriage.
You lay there wanting her as I was wanting him; similar thoughts
possessed them. Sleepless in our chaste sleeping bags, we listened

to the waves, wanting to, resisting. What part of marriage is faith?
The next night, in a guest bed in their basement, we made the baby
doctors said we were never to have. The heart's held fast by such ligaments.

Ringed by Disaster

"Daily life continued, ringed by disaster, as by a jubilant line of fire."
—*Alice Munro, "Oranges and Apples"*

She thought she'd be invisible on the evening's skin.
She should have slipped into the third row
and stayed there. Instead, when she sailed full armada
up to the front row, breasts brimming for the baby
waiting at home for her, his eyes sent up flares.
His eyes trilled and warbled, crowed, crooned
to her as if no one else were there — a Greek chorus
or wallpaper. Each night she fled home trembling,
grateful for the seatbelt's click, its authoritative steel,
to return to the husband sleeping in television's
halo. All fall she was mute stone eroding, and then
one night Bright Eyes needed a ride home because
the rain, the rain came unstoppered, and that moment,
in the windshield wipers' pulse, red and yellow lights,
refracted by all that water, kindled, and blistered, and burned.

desire

i
itself, not the satiation.
curled talons, claw and muscle,
not what they dangle over the chasm,
above the actual.
the fulminating, not the assuaging,
fomenting breaker's fury —
held breath bursting,
foam sand salt grit
ablating the beach obsolete.

ii
the consummation the spent the declawed —
how boring, how Eden.
not a breeze exhaling, not buds fattening,
not a weed.
could there even be shadow?
on the far end of the branch
the bitter unreachable crabapple.

iii
into this theater enters
snake as imagination.
not for nothing does it
meander, not for nothing
does it glint
its perfect integuments,
majestic deformation of its progress.

iv
what good does it do, this want? what
use is it, song whispered,
sweet crumb scattering?
doesn't fill the hunger,
doesn't still cacophony,
but salts a taste to wake
indifference, a furthering.

Into the White

I'd had it with Christmas. You agreed
to get away with me up the parkway
beside the Bronx River. We took the dog —
your mother said he needed a good romp,
the bad hip troubling him in winter.
The garage reminded you of the times
you'd brought back your father's latest Ford
after cruising and dragging, the tank a hair
above empty. Here, you said, pointing
to the greasy floor as if blood
had stained it — all those years spent
under a Valiant, learning how to pull an engine.

It was three-thirty, the light cold and slant.
It was snowing hard. We pulled off, parked,
the arthritic Samoyed out the car the moment
the door opened, lurching in jagged circles
to river edge and back to catch the snowballs
that splattered in his mouth. We stopped then
to listen to traffic muffled by the thick fur
of distance and followed the white dog farther
into the white meadow.

Changing the Weather

An untidy spring is bursting on the backyard hill,
landscaped ad hoc by the combination
of what was already there and what they could afford:
white Douglas iris, wet, feathered,
foxglove, hairy with promise, crowding the candy-striped azalea,
poppy volunteers. Again and again she goes to the window.
The mockingbird's come back.
There is never any money; it's a given, like seasons,
like snails that hide under the calla leaf
when the sun is hot. There is damage
to show for it. Now the clutch, the fifth
on the eleven-year-old VW that labors up the hill,
is shot. Do they fix it? A thousand bucks —
the tires too are bald — or find a way
to buy another car? Do they buy one
and give up going to the mountains?
The snapdragons cut back in November
reincarnate in a mix of pinks and creams,
and the cymbidium, the one bought dormant, cheap,
has spikes flagged with buds. They wonder
over this birth, know its name —
Buxom Lass — but not its outcome.

The job he thinks she should take would pay for the car,
another just-for-now, just-until-something-better.
Like the Jetta, she's good money after bad —
nothing sticks. Her mind floats on surfaces,
Ophelia, drowned, drifting.

They plant columbine above
the grave of the boy's hamster,
a way of teaching nothing
just ends. They try this
and that. Somewhere, butterflies
are changing the weather.

Good Housekeeping

The terracing, the feral shrubs, flagstone interruptus —
Who said what, who got the AKC-registered Dalmation?

What scenes, high words, threats and imprecations?
Tanqueray in the foxtails, lawn gone to gopher.

Call the smoker of big cigars. Mildew on the sweet peas.
Dieback, fireblight, spilled blood of roses.

Where are the barbecues of yesteryear? Oxalis in the flowerbeds,
bird nest in the bottlebrush, spreading purple loosestrife.

Crabgrass, snails, ravages of bramble. How long
has the passion vine subverted the bedroom window?

Sunshine Through Rain

after Kurosawa

The sea in the rear view mirror
in sun-bestowed light like
a pocket-polished nickel,
telephone poles, wires, and cables
holding up the canopy
of heaven, and rain
falling everywhere but,
in framed focus, on solemn
procession of foxes in human pelts —
fox groom carrying an umbrella,
fox bride, billowing skirts
gathered clear of the wet grass,
photographer motioning:
there, now *closer*, now *kiss*;
mother of the bride looking
up at the looming sky, seeing
me! Just then the thunder.
How fast can I run
— having breached the secret
ceremony — for don't I know
the foxes' wedding is not to be
witnessed by humans
and punishment will be exacted
by a righteous and wrathful god?

Darkness Visible

Was You Ever Bit by a Dead Bee?

Were you ever offered choice of a nickel or a dime,
        and did you take the nickel?
Do you ever pray to a god
        you don't believe in?
Have you ever wondered if the cow in your burger
        also had a story?
Do you wonder why we call one room
        the living room?
Have you ever visualized
        the manner of your dying?
Do you wonder if anyone at all speaks
        your language?
Do you worry that you will catch
        something incurable?
Have you figured out how
        you would escape from prison?
Have you ever worn a red coat
        with brass buttons?
Did you think he was thinking of you
        when he wrote that?
What do you think an ant on a bedsheet knows
        about geometry?

Don't Ask

after a recording by Sonny Rollins

These blues are steel gray, you ride them. Jet trails
diagonal a cobalt sky. Silk wind
　　　　whips hair across your cheek.
Metal taste between your teeth drives you.

Night drifts in with the honey scent of the viburnum.
The saxophone implores ...
　　　　At the red light, the world's on fire.
Now you climb, pressed into the curves of each turning.

Come on oh come on oh come on baby please.
From here every splintered pain finds you.
　　　　Your body aches for miracles or sleep.
Sun, like God's one eye on you, is rising.

Laboratory

The night, like a Hopper painting,
vibrates in a frequency emitted
by someone exiting the room
who packs his bags and takes
his breathing with him. His shadow
is dark green, portentous, sticky
as a web. What she might have said
is as real as words. Leaves
that she never quite sees falling
pile sodden underfoot just the same.
She should have been a writer
with her novel ending.
Is it in or out she wants? Small change
or miracles? Frogs beguiled
by water warming, loll innocent, cooked.

Guests

Crossing their pencil legs they sit
in the rafters of my dream and smoke
and ruffle filigree-veined wings
like guests gossiping among
the hors d'oeuvres in the gloom.
Still they seem at home
and flap and chat and flick
the ashes from their tiny cigarettes
and the ashes sift down, drift —
a cloud a dust a film a coat a snow
falls, and still they sit and tap,
flutter, and describe,
until the ashes blot out stars,
streetlights, all illumination, and the night
is a coffin that grows heavy and heavier
and does not let out sounds or lift.

Closing

"... the ride was so neglected that tails were falling off the horses."
(item in *San Francisco Chronicle*)

Imagine tails falling off the horses, it's that bad,
late September in the garden: freeway weeds

transporting beetles from chives to chard,
parsley all seed, snail babies maundering in lettuce—

She won't go out there to see the heart plucked
from the face of the sunflower, skeletal pea vines,

Visigoth ivy descending to plunder. Once
neat rows of new green heralded a field

of black; now the crooked fence vaults
three anachronistic roses: derelict, down

on their luck. Imagine carnival music playing,
people yawning to their cars, the empty carousel spinning.

Float

She wears the days like his mother's ring, a casual inheritance.
All summer, strands of tinsel hung behind the television.
Fall was dry, a sallow, lackluster heat. And now
a plush rain; walking in it's like drifting face down
in the green lake, a dead-man's-float kind of day,
not alive from the surface. Dormant frog-like things
lie glutinous with mud. Silent onlookers and tule reeds
sway on the periphery of vision.

She is walking the dog around the lake.
Here, a duel was fought; there's the boat house.
Empty, in ice plant and bramble, a bottle —
Miss Paula's Soothing Cough Syrup Imported
From Hong Kong. Skaters and runners and bikes
swim past her. If she holds her breath long enough,
she'll stop dreaming. How long can this last? What
would it take to break these waters?

How To:

1. Walk on Water

The secret is: don't think deep.
Don't think at all of undersea canyons
more vast than continents.
Think light, spare.
Spot a point in the distance. Dance
with new laved feet.

2. Sink

There are stones in your pockets
you put there. Sink
below the surface, passing
big daddy grouper, pouting his thick lips.
You're over your head now — there's a name for this:
bathophobia, fear of the deep,
and there's fear of failure,
floods, dampness, demons —
schools of fears, silver
as anchovies swimming.
Descend headfirst into silt,
diatomaceous earth and silicate,
shell and bone and everything
you've missed.

3. Swim

Minus stones,
your buoyancy propels you
out of the sludge, past swaying kelp,
into the medium you were born to.
Unbearable blue. Hallelujah!
You gasp, swim less fiercely now,
think: *this is easy.*
You could go on like this forever.

Medium Blue

I raise the rice paper shades to a morning moon.
I try to imagine the round world without me.

It's easy to become a sentimental song,
moist with spores like a mushroom.

Poplar leaves shiver.
Young man rides by on a bike.

I could have made him stop once,
made him sweat and stutter.

Not that I don't appreciate
red wine, cool sheets, cooking onions.

But is this how the dead feel,
unused, invisible?

Take your hand.
Put it right through my heart.

Pill

As if someone left the door open and I wandered in,
sat down. Found the porridge on the table — just right.
Watched a person in the window looking in,
followed her through the garden, the dark wood,
into a clearing flooded with god light.

I thought: life is a cloth you put on.
I shall wear this one —
a shawl, for now: cozy, warm,
like arms, like home.
If I wanted to, I could take it off.

Signed, Desperate

I am in love with a wonderful woman I was planning
to marry, but she broke it off. It's just a misunderstanding,
I'm sure. I keep all her letters in a drawer, dream of them

spilling on the floor through the mail slot, like blood
in a dream of sharks. A letter would make me forget
what I was watching on television, water would boil

to empty in the pot. Although she never wrote much:
time of arrival, flight number. I'd wait as close as I could get
to the gate with a rose. Her hair smelled like honey when I put

my lips to it. This other guy she talks about doesn't know her
like I do, could never make her smile. And you know
how young men talk. I know that when she listens to Bach,

her fingernails cut scallops in her palms. I know why small animals
frighten her. Please, tell me how to get her back. Signed, *Desperate*.
P.S. I miss the way she covers her teeth when she laughs.

Copernican Revolution

It's not about me. I've conceded my spot
in the center. There's no more to it than this:
smell of fennel over the marshes;
later, along the freeway, resinous pines.

An egret by an off ramp. A shadow on a wall.
A grace note in the air, spicy like cedar.
Words that are always there, but voices drown them.
Each morning, the infant skin of light.

Darkness Visible

for Johnny Cash

When you crawl off
        into a cave
to die
        but don't
and they won't
        show the scene
in your biopic,
        there being nothing
to see
        and no light
to see it by
        and no way
to hear
        the conversation
in the skull-cave
        with your god,

you must sing something
        keen enough
to lift the absolute
        weight of that dark
and show
        why your god
would not have you

and take with you the mute
        bound
shackled
        among us
who have no god
        into the cave-maw—
hard by: pool fingers,
        blisters,
speleogens,
        spar,
and ooze of moon milk—
        O locus empirical!
so we can know
        what you said
        what you heard.

ShBoom

Lorraine Asks Should She Have a Baby

No, don't do it. Why?
Not diapers, everything underfoot, sleep lost to teething.
None of that matters any more than the spanking of mud
from a cab spinout on your way to the interview — so you don't
get the job. After the hot bath, the tall drink, it becomes
a story to recall late at night among friends.

No, don't do it because love like this hurts
in a new way that is always with you
(like being bald on a sunny day — you can't forget your hat).
And the enemy will know the one thing
they can hold over you —
as in Orwell, *the rats*.

Life Could be a Dream (*ShBoom ShBoom*), Sweetheart

SWAK — A lipstick kiss smacks the mirror
at Tibbett's pool. Coppertone and chlorine
blue water, bubbled black asphalt.

Ingrid, the neighbor's daughter,
showing her underpants to anyone
who asks. Days like stops on a flute

through which wind blows — shouts
carried uphill. Anthony talking dirty
in the woods behind the school,

beer cans in the stream bed, cigarette
butts on a path. On the lawn, purpled
rose petals. *Jazz boys*, says Lisa,

jazz boys, and takes off her clothes
to dance. Signs in unfamiliar
language, fireflies trapped in glass,

women doing dishes in the kitchen.
Piccolo sounds under a streetlamp moon.

Mescalito

Its name was Mescalito, after Castaneda's ally,
a second-hand black Yamaha 650,
gas tank customized to up-tilt like a chopper.
No burly Harley; it was slender, wasp-waisted.
You could see its body parts: head, thorax, abdomen.

Hold on, he said. Okay, I thought —
worse ways to die than in thigh-butt embrace.
The day the roommate's neurotic mutt
shat all over the bathroom rug,
he cursed, kick started, did 80 miles an hour
up the Saw Mill — fifteen minutes
from Manhattan to Dobbs Ferry.

But sometimes on a hot, summer night,
we'd do a slow dance through Central Park,
leaning first left, then right into the curves,
so low the foot peg sparked.

Back in Yonkers

They sit in a booth at Angelo's, this pizza place
where Jim and Tom used to pick up girls from St. Barnabas
back before the war and the march against the war,

before Jim's best friend Eddy *bought it* on prom night
driving off the Tappan Zee, taking three others with him,
before that beached, sunburnt summer when Tommy

joined the Navy because it was safer than getting drafted
and going to Vietnam, and they sent him to Vietnam anyway,
before she lost her raincoat and virginity on a night filled

with incense and *In-A-Gadda-Da-Vida*. So Tommy and Jim
get heroes and Buds. She gets a slice and a Lite. She goes,
There's nothing like Yonkers pizza, and Tommy goes, *Yeah,*

and Jim who never left goes, *It's not the same these days, though.*
A few more brews and they're in the Valiant, its spray-painted
silver body like a tin pot in the moonlight. They drive up

the Bronx River Parkway, and each time they hang a right
she slides from Jim to Tommy, and each time they cop a left,
from Tom to Jim. In the parking lot they take a few tokes.

They're feeling so good when they get to Jim's, they laugh
about Otis elevators all the way to the fifth floor. When she
gets out of the bathroom Tom's on the bed, Jim's on the rug,

and she goes to Jim and they start, and then Tom's there too,
with her and Jim, when Jim's mom walks in — who won't say
anymore that she was the girl Jim should marry.

Back Pages

It must have been obvious that people who could not agree
on which booth to sit in, or which side of the booth, or who
would sit by whom — would never end up in beatific, pacific
lockstep, but that's what we swore to, that day, over Genesee
beer, in a bar that smelled of beer and piss, the end of the first
real day of summer, when it was certain the snow was gone,
and stereo speakers facing out played *Truckin'* at maximum
volume and winter's melt hung in the air, as humid as it
could get without wringing rain. We would live as family,
we said, though we didn't pin down exactly where, Kevin
dead set on a farm in Minnesota, Emily unable to tolerate
being more than a stone's throw from the ocean, Bobby,
sitting thigh to thigh with Kathy at the crystal-patterned
laminate, longing to hold Kevin's curly head in his hands,
and everyone wondering whether Tom — three beers
ahead of the pack by 9:00 — just might have a problem
with drink. Then the pizza came and another pitcher.
Summer was short and hot. By October's first snowflake,
we'd split in as many directions as pool balls break
 — though Tom still lives in town, I think.

Gal Friday

If, for instance, she had fallen to her knees
as the Vice President of Development suggested,
that afternoon with the snow falling, assuring discretion,

or even if she had wholly understood,
as he clomped his boots on the rug
and settled back, hands behind his head,

calling her into the room, that you could,
in a few minutes, alter, if not the course
of history, a river rushing to the ocean,

a story entering the sea of all the stories —
It's not as if she were ignorant of the fact:
the act of spontaneous combustion,

the spark of skin's ignition. She knew
what she knew. She was not
a beauty. She never told anyone

of the script that played over
in her daydreams and nightmares.
She must bring these things upon herself

perhaps the way she made up
her face — lips too red — or wore
no slip beneath her dress; maybe a code

she sent but could not decipher
that said how the drama would play out
and implied how it would end. Though as it was

the moment passed, the snow now
whipped fast from flurry into blizzard —
all the way home she leaned into it.

La Vie Intérieure

The Champs-Elysées along the dining room wall
narrows to a point in the distance where
green figures stroll under parasols on a field of cream
as if perspective could persuade you
of something beyond this wall
other than the boiler room churning heat.

You are the boy, slicked back, seal-black hair,
in front of the new '52 Ford —
framed forever on the Wurlitzer —
about whom they whisper they tried everything.
At night you lie tangled in sheets;
a car coughs, complains, turns over.
It will corrode with weather and rock salt
in Wanamaker's parking lot
until the tow truck comes in spring.
The air conditioner burrs on through winter.
It is Christmas. The Yule log on TV
burns and is not consumed.

Marin County Fair, Fourth of July

A knife casts a shadow on a naked back
where we wait in line for The Nightmare,
shrieks and sirens erupting
each time the doors swing wide.
A whop bop a loo op, a whop bam boom
spouts the clown mouth.
Dry grass and dust in afternoon heat rise.

A dollar will let you try your skill
at hooking a goldfish in purple water.
An Aladdin takes sixteen bull's-eyes —
thirty-two for the life-size plush tiger
with a heart on its behind.
A blond boy eating blue cotton candy
waits his turn at the Port-o-Let.

Two fifteen-year-olds, earrings adangle,
silver circling their eyes,
share caramel apples and pickles.
Above the black lace of their bras
new pink sunburns begin to shine.
They talk of the boys they will meet tonight
on the hill at the fair's east side.
The fireworks will start after dark
as will the rest of their lives.

Plummeting

All year the boy has waited to see
shooting stars, the meteor showers called the Perseids.
Perseus slew Medusa, rescued Andromeda —
but was half immortal. The gods favored him,
and Zeus, his dad, starred him in death in the sky.

The boy thinks how great it would be
to see rock burn through dark billions,
a god's eye singling him out, glowing closer,
to crash at his feet. Wouldn't the cows be startled?
He'd keep a piece as proof. He savors
the impossible odds, a hard candy
hoarded in his tongue's curl.

But they hadn't counted, his mother and father,
on summer fog, low valley clouds, the lights of the city.
They turn around, head back toward the Bay,
the event snuffed without ignition like the trip to the Sierra
they can't manage to pay for this summer.

They would have been there now, standing astonished
in cow-pied lupine while the best ever fireworks
swept through the heavens. *I saw one, I saw one!*
...two, three, four — he'd count and lose track
as he loses track now, falling into the dark sameness
of sleep in the back seat, his chance in a billion
plummeting all the way through the galaxy
to where he would have stood in that meadow.

Mary Lou Calls Me From Denver

Mary Lou calls me from Denver — snow icing
steps and sills. *Hi*, she says.
Here, it's rained for weeks, and I'm stuck in this ark.
Twelve years ago — it was summer — we sat
on Mary Lou's porch drinking beer and eating
Polish sausage; and twelve years before that
her creamy face confettied with milk chocolate freckles
turned up in the kitchen every time Mom
took something from the oven.
Mary Lou says in the phone, *I'm recovered.*
Phil's left. The twins are twelve.

I think of her girls looking as Mary Lou did,
freckled and fat in Sunday pink organza
with satin cummerbund, doing the one tap routine
she could remember — *Oh My Beautiful Doll* —
with flippy curls her sister Gail set for her.
She polished the nails too, Passion Crimson,
though Mary Lou bit them down to thin red slices of melon.

Upstairs in the room Mary Lou shared with her sister
we found the blue leatherette diary under Gail's pillow,
unlocked it with the key kept on its brass clasp,
read it together on the chenille bed,
under a Jesus with sky-blue eyes and golden halo.
We'd got to the bit where Larry stuck
his tongue in Gail's mouth, when Mary Lou
tapped me on the shoulder, pointing
out the window to the city bus.
That's the bus that ran over Daddy,
Mary Lou said. *He was skunk drunk.*
I said I was sorry. She shrugged

then as I imagine she does now, on her end
of the phone, to my murmurs applauding sobriety,
my empty offer to come and visit
if she and the twins were ever in town.
Big drops of rain tap-tap
on the chicken-wire glass skylight
above the basement stairwell.

Yetta Came Back

Yetta came back last night, Daddy,
a feathery yellow-pink bird,
spooning soft-boiled egg
from a bone china cup;
then she picked up her knitting.
We talked, being two moms,
about the hardware business,
the six sisters she brought over,
and you, last of her children,
coming twelve years after the others
when she'd just about given up
Grandpa Izzy to his chickens.
She knew you took her book
in your hands and burned it, unopened.
A foolish woman, you say. *All she cooked
was lettuce and boiled chicken.*

She never looked down
The needles clicked.
She shrugged. She knitted
because she knitted.
What does it matter who the sweater fit?

Two Bad Books

1.

Not Lorna Doone, Ivanhoe, Little Women:
classics with color plates, leather bound,
gold-lettered; I remember *The Pink Dress*,
the eponymous chiffon hanging in Donna's
closet for the day that almost didn't happen,
that boy in black leather, the furtive groping,
the hot rod, the Lovers' Lane. Such sultry weather
— she ignores the fever burning, maybe the devil's
warning. Appendicitis arrives just in the nick.
Morning. See Donna in the pink dress
at the prom with the boy her mother picks.

2.

The other book, historical fiction: or fucking
dressed up in calico and gingham. Pioneer miss
marries — first, the boy next door, who takes
her virginity and loses his scalp to Indians;
second, the perfect gentleman in bed,
who is plugged with lead when caught
holding a hand with one too many aces,
who, as luck would have it, leaves her
a silver mine; third, the cowboy brute who leaves
purple bruises on her peaches-and-cream skin.
He liked his peaches, husband number three did.

Bequest

Robyn Love You Buckets Hurry Home, Eric

in six-inch light blue characters canted upward
orbiting the lamppost, a note passed to God,
like a page ripped from the spiral binding
at back of class, as a candle lit for carved saint,
or voices chanting, spiced grains left at altar,
spelling a Holy Name, gray smoke rising
from fat slab hissing on embers. Here
lamppost is conduit, theater, intercessor.
Here writ her name where car careened,
here screams, here the smell of charred flesh
and rubber, and glass fractal radiating out
from web center. There, the fixed fact
of death at that center. Where chrysanthemum
bunch yellowed, and tied with blue ribbons,
two helium balloons bobbled, metallic, Mylar.

The Three of You

What set you off? The bike, reluctantly dragged out of storage,
that no right-minded thief would steal, the way the kids fell all over

each other going out, leaving a quiet caved in on itself — ahead of them
brightness of such magnitude there is no looking at it? Those nights

once, effervescent as cola, you, your best friend Rita, and Mike,
the whole summer the three of you pedaling around town in leather

sandals and cutoffs, sitting on the lawn under the jacaranda, on a rug
in front of the television, or watching the dawn over the reservoir,

paleness warming and gulls circling, deceived by rumors of water.
Then, breakfasts of fresh bread and sweet butter — you listened

to music while sun, like butter, dripped, and you slept together in a heap.
But Rita was alone that October, found on icy moraine where she fell.

You're on your second marriage. It's her bike you keep in storage.
The jacaranda is lush. Hush.

Peacches

Peaches

Windham House Assisted Living

The strawberry shortcake arrives: a median strip
of angel food between two red freeways,
landscaped with a Cool Whip curl.

But *fresh peaches and cream* — he misses that, you hear
him say to three gray ladies who flank his table,
to the salt and pepper, to the pastel prints on the walls.

Could he taste the words, a summer morning,
rich and sweet, sun smearing the east, dripping
its syrup onto the dark shade of leaf

as he reached up to pick the peach, warm as her
pillowed cheek, and rinsed it under the porch tap
where the milkbox held its cool, glassed treasure?

How the peaches seem to stand for everything,
and how maybe if he could taste one again, it
would be okay to die and be done.

But no, he misses *peaches*. The rest is in your mind,
you who will conclude your visit and walk off,
your life still sticky, and you in the juice and thick of it.

The First to Go

The space she takes up shrinks.
As liquid finds its level, the day's events shift to cover
the gap her departure will create.
Already she doesn't recognize her daughter
or the Jell-O they push toward her in spoons.
Maybe a week, a month —
the sister from Long Island she hasn't seen in years
shows up at the door,
the sister-in-law tries on funeral clothes.
It's as if she's already left
on a long trip; what remains
of her is a forwarding address to send postcards to.
Disconnected words arrive like broadcasts
transmitted on frequencies received
from astronauts walking on the moon.
She's moved into past tense or pause.
Memories of her are rainwater in a crack.

Mom Poem

"I read poetry to save time." — *Marilyn Monroe*

Mom and Marilyn

My mother and the Argentines loved Marilyn,
the kitten smile, the take-me glamour.
In Buenos Aires they stand in line for hours
to get to touch the shimmering green gown
beaded with six thousand rhinestones
that Marilyn wore the night she sang
her breathy happy
birthday to Kennedy.

Mom treasured a recipe from '54 —
a pineapple upside down cake —
because on the reverse of the yellowed clip
Joe DiMaggio bestows a wedding kiss
on Marilyn's inspiring lips
and on her hand, an eternity band
of 35 diamonds.

Mom Sets Foot in Another Country

Here and here, she's not allowed,
although she can just see in,
as through the windows of a house
she once lived in, in another country

where she made coffee first thing in the morning
for sixty years, and now this thing called coffee
is bird tracks on the beach, the birds themselves
departing skyward, eroding sand.

Archaeologist, she figures
how the woman in yesterday's kitchen
would stand, where she would put
the dirt-brown dust in the pot

and where the water. How
new the world is!
She tosses out the cups and saucers
after breakfast because they are used.

Mom at Sea

Mom sits on the couch where we put her,
small boat moored on a brocade ocean.
A cloud settles; each day it covers more of her face.

Mom Comes to Me in a Dream

Naugahyde on a balsa wood frame,
face down on the carpet. It's Mom,
complaining about being left in that state.
I start over to her. Yes,
it's one of those dreams
where you need a thumb's perspective
on interstellar space.

Michelangelo's God gestures toward Adam:
There they are, on the ceiling,
fingers drawing further apart —
at arm's length, so to speak,
though face to face.

Quite the gap to spark. Time
for Noah's flood and his ark,
for the multitudes in twos, and the dove
bringing back the olive. Not godforsaken,
God help me. I sit her up. It's morning.

Mom Comes to Me From Past and Future

East on 580, south I-5 and 99, I drive
The Valley, past growers' billboards
for nuts and fruit. Twenty years from now
I will see a pistachio
and think: My mother is dead.

Among rows of irrigated almonds
an old Ohlone pounding acorns on a rock
looks up across centuries
to where I pass on the Interstate.

Mom Unpacked

How my arms upraised to pull back my hair
look like my mother's. How I fold
one glove into the other so they are holding hands
and tuck the tidy package in the jacket pocket
as she would do. How when Scott says,
inoperable brain cancer this afternoon
it's Mom I see announcing at the pool
that she'd an illness to trump her friends'
arthritis, hip replacements, and cardiac infarcts.
She said it the same way she'd tell you she
was first in her class in Walton Girls Latin.
Then she tripped on the beach chair
and glared at me as I helped her up.
It's the illness, I tell myself, and the next day
at Henri's buying tomatoes: *When I want tomatoes,*
I want tomatoes, grabbing the bag from me, packing
tomatoes to outlast her. *Can't you do anything?*
They would have cried if they'd been animal.

Mom Sees a Lake

What does it look like
from there, Mom? You have
no god, no taste for fiction,
no mortar to brick immortal story.
We hang on to your words,
to any indication of soaring
above this bed.

Mom Asks, Doves Assent

After a while, there's nothing to say.
Mourning doves have built a nest
in the locust at the end of the terrace
after a short courtship. You wait on your back
in the small bed of your marriage,
propped on pillows, for instructions.
How does one die? — bit by bit,
but it takes practice. Your whole life
you sharpened your pencils, did your lessons.
Good, say the doves,
good, good, good, good girl.

What Khadem Said

In Bangladesh, you get used to death.
When the river floods, we work 20 hours
a day, burying the bodies seven to a grave,
tying petrol-soaked rags around nose and mouth
to drown the other smell; you are numb
for hours when you take it off. When I looked

out the window at University one afternoon
and saw two groups advancing, it was just
another day — the usual gunshots. I thought,
again, this will spoil my lesson. Then, in the courtyard,
half a dozen feet away, one of my students, the surprised
look on his face as a bullet burst between his eyes;

a crow swooped down then, catching up his brain.
I was only a boy when we buried my father.
I got down into his grave. It was my job
(eldest son, *son of Islam*) to turn his face
to Mecca. I took his head in my two hands —
at first it would not yield — and snapped it into place.

The Year the Fathers Went Missing

We hardly noticed at first, despite the indelible
thumbprints on skull tissue, the intricate scars
and excoriations on that muscle called the heart.

It was exceptionally quiet: a lack of lamentation,
an absence of rending. There was the guilt, of course,
its themes and variations, its lulls and crescendos.

But no graceful manumission or even an ending.
Just all that nothing. And then the dream, this:
the benign, nondescript beings we passed

the heavy jars to on the stairs; a fluid motion, matter-
of-fact and momentous. With each transfer, the pull
lessened, the toll on our claim was not as large.

Analyst and theologian argue what it meant.

Bequest

1.

He'd be back in a month, Jacques thought,
long before the winter wheat ripened
for harvesting, before *V*-forms of geese
lifted off Superior pointed toward the Gulf.
In his head he saw it — Marie in the kitchen
ladling soup, the youngest of nine on her hip.
He would make her hand a cup to hold
nuggets big as quails' eggs
that the Klondike had washed up to him.

2.

Seven years later, he pushes
open the kitchen door, stopping to tap
slush and mud from his boots,
walks to the head of the table, sits down.

3.

Luc stands a moment in the dark barn.
Dottie meets his gaze with chocolate eyes, Choux-Choux
the calf nuzzling her pink teats. Good.
For a while last night he'd feared for both,
lying near her, steam rising from her breath and his
as her side heaved and the calf started to descend.
One hand inside the cow, the other kneading belly,
turned the calf round, something he'd never done
or seen, although he'd heard tell of it —
a victory of luck and will, the kind they'd come to depend on.
He pushes open the kitchen door, stopping to tap
slush and mud from his boots …
      Papa?
Yes.
      Things have changed.
The boy's hand grips the chair where his father sits.
The old man gets up, walks to the window.
Ten pair of eyes glue to him. He turns
toward the blurred hills beyond the isinglass,
a lump the size of seven years in his throat.
Scrrch, scrrch of metal spoon on the empty pot.

Heron as Ghost

...The wait's begun again,
The long wait for the angel,
For that rare, random descent.
— Sylvia Plath

Each blade in the wide meadow this morning gleams,
and Pine Lake, shallow as a plate, reflects all hope.
A great blue heron lands across the pond.
It's like a ghost, you say, the heron. You can
just make it out behind the tule reeds.
Its long legs look just like tule reeds,
and it moves in and out of view
with an awkward grace, like beings move
into this life or death. It seems to mean something
that it comes here, as if it comes to us,
this large bird with a taste for freshwater crayfish,
all the way from Bolinas to this city pond.
Its blue is insubstantial. It is alone.
It does not see us. It has its own requisites.

Angle of Reflection

In the nickel blue haze of late December, a freighter
ghosts past smoky hills into the mouth of the Bay,
sun washing stucco citrus, leaving shadows purple.

It shines: on a man lying on a sofa by a west window,
sweatered wing over his sleep-soft face —
in his dream, a small boy wanders the city
with a ball, looking for others to play —

and on a woman in a kitchen — she picks up pieces
of a cup, translucent porcelain,
as if they were her mother's bones and sweeps
the rest into the trash beneath the sink.

And the last low angle of light falls
on a television left on, no one watching the drama,
and on the lily in a vase, making it holy,
its creamy pink petals, its bleeding heart.

Small Talk

Small Talk

Not the news at ten, policy and paradigm,
but murmurs at night at a border, first
syllables of newborn, not the general's
orders, but your name in the mouth
of a lover, words that make you cry
all night at sixteen, turn ice into water,
whispered at a fence — small but its sharp
tongue pricks you like sun on the hairs
of your forearms a moment around noon
on a day toward the end of winter.

Freeloaders

We are all freeloaders under God.
— *Uncle Vanya,* Anton Chekhov

The great man lived in a hotel room; nothing
on the wall. On the sink a straight razor,
boar's-bristle brush, cake of soap in a thick-walled cup.

After the incident at the P.O., postal workers
pick up the mail and deliver it as addressed,
spotted with blood of their coworkers.

A dream of two boxes; you could see inside either,
but not both. She had no interest in the box that held
the past. He had none in the box that held the future.

Redwing blackbirds at a lake, a sudden flare
of knowledge, a clarity, erupting —
revelation, but you could not say what.

Two-year-old drowns in the backyard pool,
mother deciding what to defrost for dinner.
You tongue her pain until it possesses you.

The lover's footprints in the snow lead away
from the house, ice over. Snow melts to grass,
yields to corn and the deep hum of summer.

Wolves, normally shy of the geometries
of man, risk everything when their pups hunger.
That degree of need in the blood drove her.

Sparrows in the Acacia

You walk down a sidewalk at dusk.
Yellow eyes of houses contain children
setting dinner, cataract with steam.

If home is an abstraction like God,
it gathers sparrows in the acacia.
A boy inside the bus and his father,

outside, matching hands on cold glass,
the shearing fact of loss.
A tug chest-deep makes the throat tighten,

tears freshen, let down.
Dusk gathers and knots into dark.
Heels clop on pavement

and the cold muscles on.
Through the smell of wood fires burning,
the kelp-brine air, you hear sirens,

dark-haired mothers keening.
If God is a place like home,
it is a landmark to steer by.

At night, the sparrows are silent;
the stone in your pocket,
its almost perfect roundness a prayer.

We Catch a Trout

Here he is: skinny, adolescent, speckled, staring
up at us from the almond-studded aluminum pan.
He is lovely but so hard to eat.

From across the lake you shout. I watch
the triumphant heave as you reel him in.
When I catch up, you're removing the hook from his lip.

Suddenly … *Get him, get him!* I yell as he flips,
all volition and muscle.
He'd be back in the lake in one more flip.

But you do get him.
You look at me: *I'll have to kill him.*
You take him by the tail and hit, hit, hit.

You put him down and he flings
himself next to the water.
So you take a rock. That does the trick.

Sleep Happens

Isn't it remarkable how sleep happens,
its magnanimity? — how even the cruelest
of despots can be nightly found
curled in its caress, this tender,
thumb-to-face baby, though his mother
would likely not recognize
the bruised hand, dried blood,
the spittle at the corner of the mouth
where the breath flutes, meted,
and possibly his dreams are halcyon
and golden as any creature's awed
by the generosity of breasts and afloat
in sleep's affluent ocean? He stirs,
he relives, he considers — what?
And day seeps slowly back,
with its whispered smoke, its stink
of purpose, with its acrid moans,
its explosive dialect of fists.

Studying Forgiveness

She doesn't know quite what to look for —
something more than the assumption,
based on Newton's law,
that for every action there's an equal,

tit for tat — right and wrong
served like ping, like pong returning.
She learns how the heart empties
and fills, opening its chambers,

flood and reflux, deluge subsiding,
to take what's given, the sharp edges
of witness and proof
smoothed by tide and decision —

into a sandy beach, alien and clean
as the first fin-legged fish ever crawled upon.

The Fat Boy Jumps

The fat boy jumps into the green-brown lake,
his cannonball behind landing splat
on the viscous stillness, the rising parabola
of the splash twinning his arc of entry.
A thousand drops mirror a sun that has shone
on him twelve lavish, sultry summers, and the lily pads
and murky shapes of plump polliwogs
that swim in their tangle, and dragonflies
that hover in the hot air.
       A second jump —
as he hefts his weight, tucking his legs
and holding them to his chest,
and head back, bellows, *Geronimo!*
he has become, to the watcher on the shore,
emblem of boys, summer, lakes, and America.
       But he does not know this
as he erupts into air, mouth stretched
into an *O,* and, cheeks distended, dog paddles,
and shakes the water off his hair.

Lucy in the Sky, 6 A.M., Montgomery Street

Lucy takes off her shoes, buries her toes in robin's egg blue
wall-to-wall virgin wool carpet. They've been doing
corporate securities, mortgages, deeds of trust
since two o'clock yesterday afternoon. She yawns
at her screen, at the left-on-empty carafe of coffee,
at the Chinese take-out: cold, congealed. Stretching,
she walks to the window, envisions mute impact of bones
on pavement, police, ambulance, people scurrying —
a silent movie. Chester chews a twenty-five-dollar cigar,
peers out through his telescope, playing George C. Scott
playing Patton. He calls to her. A phone rings. The fax
is in from L.A. Outside plate glass twenty-three stories
above Chinatown, morning breaks east of Oakland:
Like sap to capillary action, elevators rise.

Five Days on Twenty

Monday
She looks out at the fabulous confectionery of man, two bridges in alignment, and in the foreground a herd of gantry cranes, bowing and pawing.

Tuesday
Today even the closer bridge is hardly discernible through a powdery haze. She has begun to gauge the quality of the day on visibility, as if the view from the 20th floor is indicative of a vision like that of a saint's, several days into a fast.

Wednesday
Down below, three emerald-headed mallards, pub crawlers out looking for a dame.
— *Gotta trawl if you want to catch anything*, says one.
— *Well, it passes the time.*
— *Quack.*

Thursday
The morning had started out fine; deep orange sorbets of sunrise, the tart-sweet air impelling her onward. Then the heat breathed on her; the air grew dense and muffled. She was a being from another planet, unused to our atmosphere. Here, among the lithe-limbed skaters in the day, she was uncoordinated and squat. A kind of vertigo came over her, and she thought she could erase herself with her hands.

Friday
Anxiety free floats in a brown haze over the city. Her skin a permeable membrane, she finds it hard to breathe. It ratchets up a notch. God, for a cool hand. In the office next door, two people are installing software. She hears them speak of *longing*. It sounds like *longing, an easy install.*

Night Vision

One notch at a time, you ratchet skyward,
as if you could crack this ceramic-plate black
with your infrared spark. You can see
in the dark, not one sly star winking.
You're so smart, you think you can untangle

the infrastructure of heaven. Experts report
the glow of all our galaxies slips
through the runcible universe,
its sum beige, not turquoise.
But you knew that, didn't you?

Wouldn't you be a better person
in a turquoise universe, content
with consanguinity, letting
spiders clutter up corners,
helping old women transcend

to the other side — cheerful, taking
a shine to the spectrum, and oh so
semiprecious? What will you do
with your newfound skill in your next
incarnation? Admire your reflection

in the retinas of wildcats? Can you see
the moiré pattern of their fears? What then,
when prey turns to hunter, gnaws
at the whitebrittle hard chipped femur
where scent of flesh still adheres?

Fraught with Danger

Let's put it this way: it's so unlikely that you ever were born.
All those stars in the sky and just one glove
to catch them. How thin the crust between foot
and fall, looming the boot that stubs out
civilization. I'm not scared, just wary,
and not of germs that lurk downtown
in old gum and expectoration
(hungry hands springing forth
as if sidewalks were Candyland
and you the Big Rock Candy Mountain) —
it's the universe that's out to get us and, what's worse,
the sky really is falling, falling apart,
matter and energy expanding to sameness.
No safety in numbers, heaven won't hold us.
Though for now the horizon holds steady,
the tree breathes through its bark.

As It Never Was

The orange moon watching the fields
augurs a good harvest. Small children
unfurl ribbons and clap away crows.
The sky is painted lapis lazuli.
Evening: white-throated swifts cut the air
with their tails. They mate, fall,
uncouple right before they would
crash to earth. We drink apple beer
and sleep. In the distance
bells toll. Summers, we journey
to the mainland. Once, on our return,
pink and silver dolphins leapt
among the long oars as we rowed.

Acknowledgments

The author wishes to thank the editors of the following journals, websites, and anthologies, in which these poems previously appeared, sometimes in earlier versions: *Bellingham Review, Best New Poets 2005, Connotation Press, Crazyhorse, Field, Hayden's Ferry Review, In Vivo, New England Review, Nimrod International Journal, North American Review, Poetry Daily, The Scripter, Switched-on Gutenberg, Tar River Review, Third Coast, Valparaiso Review,* and Zyzzyva.

Conjugated Visits is a product of much sweat, many tears, and more than a few years. Gratitude goes first to John, my love and my husband. I'd also like to thank my son Nathaniel for his love and support.

Robert Hass, his gorgeous mind and generous spirit, has for many years been a bedrock inspiration. Thank you to Brigit Pegeen Kelly — so brilliant and so kind — for nurturing this manuscript. Dorianne Laux was an early reader of this book before it was this book, and I thank her.

At Bread Loaf 2000, Yusef Komunyakaa's insightful comments challenged me, and Jill Alexander Essbaum encouraged me. More recently, poet-bloggers Charles Jensen, Peter Pereira, and Eduardo Corral have given criticism and support. Thank you to Fred Marchant for his assurances.

I am grateful for the friendship of Scott Reid Serkes, with whom I started the poetry group that now calls itself Thirteen Ways. Thank you to every member of that group, past and present — specifically, Lisa Gluskin Stonestreet and Beverly Burch, savvy readers of my manuscript, and Robert Thomas, *il miglior fabbro* and dearest friend, who read this book a thousand times.

I also thank B.H. Fairchild and *Nimrod International Journal's* Francine Ringold for the selection of "Mom Poem" for second place in the *Nimrod / Hardman Pablo Neruda Award*. It later went on to inclusion in *Best New Poets 2005*.

I am grateful for residencies at Vermont Studio Center and Virginia Center for the Creative Arts that have given me time and space to write.

About the Author

Diane Kirsten Martin was born in The Bronx and grew up just north of that, in Yonkers, New York. Her work has appeared in numerous journals, in print and online. She was awarded second place in the *Nimrod* /Hardman Pablo Neruda Prize competition, judged by B.H. Fairchild, in 2004, and was nominated for and included in *Best New Poets 2005*. In 2006, she was semifinalist in the "Discovery"/ *The Nation* competition. She has received a Pushcart Special Mention. Her poem "Hue and Cry" won first prize in the Erskine J. Poetry prize awarded by *Smartish Pace*.

Diane has a B.A. in English from the University of Rochester and an M.A. in English, Concentration in Creative Writing, from San Francisco State University. In the 1980s, Diane cofounded the group that is now the 13 Ways poetry workshop. Diane has been a fellow at Vermont Studio Center (2002) and Virginia Center for the Creative Arts (2009) and has attended Squaw Valley Community of Writers, Napa Valley Writers Conference, and Bread Loaf Writers Conference. She has taught poetry workshops for City College Continuing Education and has given many readings.

Diane works as a technical editor and writer. She lives in San Francisco with her husband, John, and her dog, Greta Garbo.